WOMEN OF MYTHOLOGY

GODDESSES, WARRIORS, AND HUNTERS

HELEN OF TROY

Ann Poeschel

Cavendish Square

New York

Published in 2020 by Cavendish Square Publishing, LLC
243 5th Avenue, Suite 136, New York, NY 10016

First Edition

Library of Congress Cataloging-in-Publication Data

Names: Poeschel, Ann, author.
Title: Helen of Troy / Ann Poeschel.
Description: First edition. | New York : Cavendish Square, 2020. | Series: Women of mythology: goddesses, warriors, and hunters | Audience: Grades: 1-4. | Includes bibliographical references and index.
Identifiers: LCCN 2019015201 (print) | LCCN 2019017765 (ebook) | ISBN 9781502651358 (ebook) | ISBN 9781502651341 (library bound) | ISBN 9781502651327 (pbk.) | ISBN 9781502651334 (6 pack)
Subjects: LCSH: Helen, of Troy, Queen of Sparta--Juvenile literature. | Mythology, Greek--Juvenile literature.
Classification: LCC BL820.H45 (ebook) | LCC BL820.H45 P63 2020 (print) | DDC 398.20938/02--dc23
LC record available at https://lccn.loc.gov/2019015201

Editor: Kristen Susienka
Copy Editor: Alex Tessman
Associate Art Director: Alan Sliwinski
Designer: Christina Shults
Production Coordinator: Karol Szymczuk
Photo Research: J8 Media

The photographs in this book are used by permission and through the courtesy of:
Cover Universal Images Group North America LLC/Alamy Stock Photo; p. 4 De Morgan Collection, courtesy of the De Morgan Foundation/Bridgeman Images; p. 6 DeAgostini/Getty Images; p. 8 Photo Josse/Leemage/Getty Images; p. 9 Acquired by Henry Walters with the Massarenti Collection, 1902, Walters Art Museum/Wikimedia Commons/File:Dutch-Portrait of the Poet Homer-Walters 37646.jpg/ CC BY-SA 3.0; p. 10 Chronicle/Alamy Stock Photo; p. 11 Fanatic Studio/Getty Images; p. 12 Dinosmichail/ Alamy Stock Photo; p. 15 Look and Learn/Bridgeman Images; p. 16 National Archaeological Museum/ Luisa Ricciarini/Bridgeman Images; p. 18 Opachevsky Irina/Shutterstock.com; p. 20 Look and Learn/ Bridgeman Images; p. 24 Ham House, Surrey, UK/National Trust Photographic Library/Bridgeman Images; p. 26 The CW/Courtesy Everett Collection; p. 28 Bruce, Ralph/Look and Learn/Bridgeman Images.

Printed in the United States of America

TABLE OF CONTENTS

Evelyn de Morgan painted this picture of Helen in 1898.

CHAPTER ONE

THE STORY OF HELEN

Helen of Troy is an important woman in Greek **mythology**. She was a **demigod**. This means she was half human and half god. She was the daughter of a god named Zeus and a human named Leda. Zeus ruled all the gods and goddesses on Mount Olympus. Leda was the queen of Sparta, an ancient **city-state** in Greece.

Helen grew up to be a very beautiful woman. Some people called her the most beautiful woman in the world. Today, people still talk about her beauty and **courage**.

Helen of Sparta

When Helen was a young woman, she married a prince named Menelaus. They became the king and queen of Sparta. One

This painting shows Paris kidnapping Helen from Sparta. A god of love targets them with his bow in the top left corner.

day, a visitor from the city of Troy arrived. The visitor's name was Paris, and he was a prince of Troy.

Paris thought Helen was the most beautiful woman he'd ever seen. He kidnapped her and took her back to Troy. When Menelaus found out she was missing, he wanted her back. He decided to go to Troy to get her. He asked other Greek leaders and their armies to join him.

The Trojan War

The Greeks and the Trojans fought over Helen. This fight was called the Trojan War, and it lasted ten years. The Greeks

The Greeks won the Trojan War by entering the city in a large wooden horse (*center*).

won the war. They came up with a plan to sneak in to Troy with a large wooden horse. After the war was won, Helen went back to Sparta.

HOMER AND THE *ILIAD*

Homer was a poet who lived a long time ago in ancient Greece. He wrote a long poem about the Trojan War. The name of this poem is the *Iliad*. It is an epic poem, which is a long story about important heroes.

This portrait shows the Greek poet Homer.

Who's to Blame?

The goddess Aphrodite is sometimes blamed for starting the Trojan War. She's the goddess of love and beauty. Some stories say she made Paris and Helen fall in love with each other.

Paris chooses Aphrodite (*in pink*) as the fairest goddess in this image.

Helen is famous because she was said to have caused the Trojan War. This war was the first time all of the Greek city-states had come together as one country. Her story is important because it was believed that the Trojan War united Greece.

ANOTHER STORY: SITA OF INDIA

Sita is a goddess in Hindu mythology. Hinduism is a religion from India. Her story is like Helen's story.

Rama and Sita are part of Indian mythology.

Sita was the daughter of Mother Earth. She was found as a baby by a king and queen and raised as a princess. Sita was married to a god named Rama. She and Rama were very happy together. Sita was a good and **noble** wife and was very beautiful.

One day, Sita was kidnapped by an evil god named Ravana. Rama fought to get Sita back. He defeated Ravana. After, he and Sita could live together again as husband and wife.

Ancient Greeks thought the gods and goddesses lived on Mount Olympus.

CHAPTER TWO

GREEK MYTHS AND LIFE

The ancient Greeks told many myths. Their myths helped explain everyday life, like lightning, thunder, fire, and earthquakes. Myths became part of Greek religion. Greeks used these stories to decide what was good and what was bad. The tales talked about heroes, gods, goddesses, and people doing surprising things.

Gods in Myths

A lot of Greek myths talked about the gods and goddesses on Mount Olympus. In Greek mythology, gods and goddesses spent time with humans on Earth. Sometimes they were nice to humans. Other times they were unkind or played tricks on them.

Life in Sparta

Sparta was a **warrior** society in Greece. The army was the most important part of Sparta. All men trained to be soldiers. They began learning at age seven.

Sparta was a special city because men and women were more equal than in other

Spartan soldiers were fierce warriors. This painting shows a Spartan army attacking.

Plays

The Greeks invented different kinds of plays. They performed the plays in large outdoor theaters. Some plays were based on Greek myths.

cities. The Spartans liked both men and women to be strong.

This statue shows a Spartan woman. She has strong arms and legs.

Spartan women had independence. They could own land, go to school, and take part in sports contests. In fact, women often danced or wrestled to show how talented or strong they were.

Women from other cities couldn't do these things. In other parts of Greece, women didn't have the same freedom as men.

Spartan girls didn't fight in wars, but they learned about war and fighting. They were supposed to be strong too.

Remembering Helen

Helen was said to have lived in Sparta at a time called the Age of Heroes. This was when Greeks thought the gods or demigods walked on Earth. This was over three thousand years ago!

Because Helen's father was believed to have been a god, the Spartans thought Helen was a goddess. However, she wasn't **immortal**. When Helen died, the Spartans worshipped her. They were proud that Helen had once been a queen of their city.

WHAT ROLE DID WOMEN PLAY?

This is a statue of Nike, the goddess of victory. She is holding a wreath.

Women were main characters in the myths of ancient Greece. They were goddesses, demigods, and humans. Each woman in these myths was special. Some were good, and some were evil. They played important and powerful roles in stories. Some women helped heroes, some fought them, and some tricked them.

In Greek stories, women were goddesses of things like love and beauty, but they could also be goddesses of things like war, hunting, and victory. The goddesses in Greek mythology were just as powerful as the gods. Some of them were even more powerful!

Spartans liked strong women. They thought Helen had been strong and beautiful. They thought she was was brave too because she stayed strong even after Paris kidnapped her.

The Spartans built a temple, or religious building, to Helen. People could celebrate her there. Young girls wanted to be beautiful and brave like Helen. They danced at the temple, thinking if they did they would grow up to be like her.

Winner of the Olympics

The first woman ever to win the ancient Olympic Games was a Spartan princess! Her name was Cynisca. She won a victory crown in 396 BCE.

This image shows Helen and others watching Paris, Menelaus, and their armies fight in the Trojan War.

CHAPTER THREE

HELEN TODAY

Helen of Troy and the Trojan War is one of the most famous stories from Greek mythology. It's told in ancient books and in today's times in new ways by different authors. Helen is also still important today because of her strength and beauty. She's a role model for women all over the world.

Helen Lives On

Stories about Helen and other myths are still taught in schools today. Students read epic poems to learn about Helen's story. They also learn about the gods and goddesses of Greek mythology.

Ancient Greece inspired modern life in many ways. For example, some English words come from Greek words, like "hero" (*íroas*) and "school" (*scholeío*).

Another Story of Helen

Another story about Helen said she was the daughter of Zeus and a goddess named Nemesis. This meant Helen was not a demigod but a goddess. She was raised by humans.

Helen in Art

Helen still shows up in art, in books, in movies, and on television. There's even a company named Helen of Troy! It makes many different items, including beauty products, shampoo, and perfume.

Helen is a popular person for artists to paint. Many famous artists like Leonardo da Vinci and Salvador Dalí have painted Helen and her story. These paintings show different events in her life. Some also imagine the story of Paris kidnapping Helen. These paintings are in museums all over the world.

A painter named Guido Reni painted this picture of Helen of Troy in the 1600s.

Writing About Helen

Homer wasn't the only poet who wrote about Helen. Other famous writers like Euripides from ancient Greece and Christopher Marlowe from England retold Helen's tale in their plays and poems. Today, authors still like to tell her story.

Helen also appears in new books about Greek gods and goddesses. Her myth has also been retold in books for kids and adults, like the *Princesses of Myth* series and the *Starcrossed* trilogy. In addition, the *Iliad* is now also a graphic novel. Its detailed pictures help tell the ancient story.

HELEN GOES TO THE MOVIES

Many movies and TV shows like to tell Helen's story in new ways. She's still a part of stories about heroes. In 2017, a show called *DC's Legends of Tomorrow* had an episode about Helen of Troy called "Helen Hunt." In it, Helen starts a war between two big movie companies, just like she did with Greece and Troy.

Helen is seen here on *Legends of Tomorrow.*

Some movies have imagined the Trojan War. In 2004, a movie called *Troy* was made about this historical event. Many famous actors starred in it. More TV shows have imagined parts of the Trojan War, like sneaking in the Trojan Horse to win the war.

Helen as a Role Model

Helen is remembered today as the most beautiful woman in the world. She was more than just beautiful, though. She's also remembered as a strong and powerful woman, and young people can look up to her today.

Myth, Fable, or Folktale?

A myth is often a story about gods or goddesses. A fable is a short story that teaches a lesson. It usually has animals as main characters. A folktale is a story that's passed down through the years in a culture. All three tell the history of a group of people. They mix real and imaginary ideas to tell the story.

Helen was brave and strong when she was taken from Sparta.

GLOSSARY

city-state A city that acts as a smaller country. It has its own government, military, and rulers.

courage The ability to do something that scares you; bravery.

demigod Someone who is the son or daughter of a human and a god or goddess.

immortal Able to live forever.

mythology A collection of stories that explains the history of a group of people, usually having gods and goddesses in it.

noble Good and honest.

warrior A brave and good soldier or fighter.

FIND OUT MORE

Books

Loewen, Nancy. *Helen of Troy Tells All: Blame the Boys*. Minneapolis, MN: Picture Window Books, 2014.

McMullan, Kate. *Hit the Road, Helen!* Minneapolis, MN: Stone Arch Boooks, 2013.

Website

Apr 24, 1184 BCE: Fall of Troy

www.nationalgeographic.org/thisday/apr24/fall-troy/history/greece/greek-gods

Video

Drawn History: The Trojan War

www.youtube.com/watch?v=TOAraslCkgU

INDEX

Page numbers in **boldface** refer to images. Entries in **boldface** are glossary terms.

ABOUT THE AUTHOR

Ann Poeschel is from El Dorado, Kansas. She received her bachelor's in English from the University of Kansas. She loves to travel and experience new cultures. In her spare time, she is a volunteer reading coach. In 2017, she earned her master's degree in publishing from Edinburgh Napier University in Edinburgh, Scotland. Her favorite stories to read are myths and fairy tales.